AVOIDING DEATH TAXES

*You Can't Take It With You,
But You Need Not Pay the Government To Die*

Raymond E. Saunders
Joseph A. Zarlengo
David L. Reich
Ted A. Koester

Partners
Lawrence, Kamin, Saunders & Uhlenhop, L.L.C.

Copyright © 2014 Lawrence, Kamin, Saunders & Uhlenhop, L.L.C.
All rights reserved.
ISBN: 1502780674
ISBN-13: 978-1502780676

AVOIDING DEATH TAXES

TABLE OF CONTENTS

The Authors ii

Acknowledgements vii

Introduction 1

Chapter I   Core Principles 4

Chapter II   Planning For Estates Under $10,680,000 14

Chapter III   Valuation 23

Chapter IV   The Grand Slam: Sale to a Defective Trust 27

Chapter V   Family Limited Partnerships 32

Chapter VI   The Charitable Deduction 36

Chapter VII   Life Insurance 44

Chapter VIII   Retirement Accounts 49

Chapter IX   A Potpourri of Other Weapons in Your Arsenal 55

Conclusion 63

THE AUTHORS

Raymond E. Saunders

Contact Information
Raymond E. Saunders, Partner
Lawrence, Kamin, Saunders & Uhlenhop, L.L.C.
300 South Wacker Drive, Suite 500
Chicago, IL 60606
  Phone: 312-924-4243
  Email: resaunders@LKSU.com
  Website: www.LKSU.com

Practice Areas
Income Tax
Estate and Gift Tax
Mergers and Acquisitions

Education
Northwestern University School of Law, J.D., *cum laude*, 1956
  Order of the Coif, Editor, *Northwestern University Law Review*
Northwestern University, B.S., Accounting, *cum laude*, 1953

Honors
Illinois Silver Medal, 1954 CPA Examination - second-highest
  grade in Illinois
Elijah Watt Sells Award, 1954 CPA   Examination – top ten
  highest grades in   United States

Bar Admissions
State of Illinois

Professional Memberships & Affiliations
Adjunct Professor, Northwestern University School of Law–
  Structuring Transactions – Purchase and Sale of a Business
Chicago Bar Association

THE AUTHORS

Joseph A. Zarlengo

Contact Information
Joseph A. Zarlengo, Partner
Lawrence, Kamin, Saunders & Uhlenhop, L.L.C.
300 South Wacker Drive, Suite 500
Chicago, IL 60606
  Phone: 312-924-4247
  Email: jzarlengo@LKSU.com
  Website: www.LKSU.com

Practice Areas
Estate Planning - Business & Corporations

Family Counselor
Thirty years of legal and tax experience combined with an amiable personality has made Joe an outstanding consigliere in reconciling opposing views in stressful family and business differences.

Education
New York University School of Law, L.L.M. Taxation, 1986
The John Marshall Law School, J.D., 1985
California State University, B.A., 1982

Honors
The John Marshall Law School, J.D., 1985, High Distinction;
  Law Review Honors; National Moot Court Competitor;
  Mugel Tax Competition—4th best brief, 1985 Quarterfinals

Bar Admissions & Court Admissions
American Bar Association, Illinois State Bar Association,
Chicago Bar Association – United States Tax Court

Professional Memberships & Affiliations
South Suburban Estate Planning Council, 1992-present
Society of Trust and Estate Planning Practitioners (STEP) 2011-present

Community Service
Chicago Volunteer Legal Services, Member 1992-present
Knights of Columbus Council, No. 9770 – Presently: Co-Chair,
  Annual Fund Raising for Special Needs Citizens –
  Previously held position: Grand Knight

THE AUTHORS

David L. Reich

Contact Information
David L. Reich, Partner
Lawrence, Kamin, Saunders & Uhlenhop, L.L.C.
300 South Wacker Drive, Suite 500
Chicago, IL 60606
  Phone: 312-924-4246
  Email: dreich@LKSU.com
  Website: www.LKSU.com

Practice Areas
Businesses & Corporations
Estate Planning
Real Estate

Education
Northwestern University School of Law, J.D., 1991
Indiana University, B.S., Finance, 1985

Bar Admissions
State of Illinois

Court Admissions
United States District Courts
Northern District of Illinois

Professional Memberships & Affiliations
Adjunct Professor, Northwestern University School of Law—
  Structuring Transactions – Purchase and Sale of a Business
Chicago Bar Association
Israel Cancer Research Fund, Board of Directors
Modestus Bauer Foundation, Board of Directors
Highland Park Community Foundation, Board of Directors

THE AUTHORS

Ted A. Koester

Contact Information
Ted A. Koester, Partner
Lawrence, Kamin, Saunders & Uhlenhop, L.L.C.
300 South Wacker Drive, Suite 500
Chicago, IL 60606
  Phone: 312-924-4257
  Email: tkoester@LKSU.com
  Website: www.LKSU.com

Practice Areas
Business and Corporations
Estate Planning
Real Estate
Probate and Trust Administration

Client Advocate
With 16 years of experience as a lawyer, Ted brings a pragmatic and preventative approach to developing comprehensive and cost-effective solutions for clients.

Education
Seton Hall University, School of Law, J.D., 1998
Eastern Illinois University, B.S., Financial Management, 1994

Bar Admissions
State of Illinois
State of Wisconsin

Professional Memberships & Affiliations
American Bar Association
Illinois Bar Association - Trust & Estates Section
Chicago Bar Association - Trust Law Committee Member,
  Probate Committee Member, Speaker
Chicago Estate Planning Council - Board Member June 2013-Present,
  Speaker
Seton Hall Alumni Association - Chicago Chapter Board Member
  & President
National Business Institute - Speaker

Acknowledgements

Even though we have four co-authors, we could not have completed this book without valuable assistance from others. Marcia Rollins, a legal assistant with our law firm for more than thirty years, laboriously typed and retyped the many drafts, and in doing so corrected numerous errors. Another of our legal assistants, Anna Strelka, an accomplished author in her own right, did the final editing of this book and used her superior grammatical skills to improve the final language. Anna also made all of the necessary final arrangements, including formatting, printing, selection of the cover, and others. We doubt that any of the authors could have accomplished these final details.

Inez Saunders, who is Ray's wife, contributed the subtitle "You Can't Take It With You." That expression is one that she has repeatedly used in conversations with Ray in considering possible extravagances.

The credit for the idea to write this book belongs to Joe's good friend, Gary Klaben of Coyle Financial Counsel, Inc. He not only came up with the idea, but he also provided the technique for doing this quickly and easily. We are grateful to Gary.

We also acknowledge our gratitude to each of you who read this book. Although portions might be technical and not very exciting, we hope that reading this will provide you with valuable insight that will benefit you in planning your estate.

We will welcome hearing your comments.

INTRODUCTION

Will medical science unlock the secret for humans to achieve immortality? Will the legal profession and society abandon the centuries-old principles that control the passage of property at death? Since neither of these is likely to occur during your lifetime, you need an estate plan.

A Capsule History

The first known inheritance tax of which we have knowledge dates back to ancient Egypt as early as 700 B.C. More recently, in 1796, Great Britain introduced "death taxes" in order to finance its war against Napoleon.

In the United States of America, the inception of the federal estate tax as we know it occurred in 1916, but there were previous tax statutes imposing "death taxes." The Stamp Act of 1797 required the purchase of federal stamps for wills and other probate documents. The Revenue Act of 1862 imposed an inheritance tax (in addition to a stamp tax) on personal property received by a legatee at rates ranging from 0.75% on bequests to ancestors, descendants and siblings to 5% on bequests to distant relatives, unrelated individuals and charities. Bequests to a

INTRODUCTION

surviving spouse were exempt. Bequests and gifts of real estate were taxed beginning in 1864. In 1871-1872, following the end of the Civil War, these taxes were repealed. In order to raise revenue for the Spanish American War, in 1898 a legacy tax was enacted with tax rates ranging from 0.75% to 15%, but only on personal property. This tax was repealed in 1902.

What Is A "Death Tax"?

An estate tax is a tax that is imposed on and measured by the wealth left by the decedent. An inheritance tax (or legacy tax) is measured by the amount received by a beneficiary of a decedent. Death taxes may refer to either the estate tax or inheritance tax, or both.

In order to finance the expansion of United States governmental agencies, the 20th century produced a dramatic rise in taxation. In 1913, the Sixteenth Amendment to the Constitution permitted the enactment of the federal income tax, which was immediately enacted that same year. The Revenue Act of 1916 imposed an estate tax on net estates in excess of $50,000. The estate tax rates were graduated from 1% on the first $50,000 to 10% on the excess above $5.0 million. The gift tax was enacted in 1924 and became a permanent part of the federal tax system in 1932.

The impact of the federal estate and gift tax system on individuals is very narrow. Estate tax returns are filed for less than 2% of all adult deaths, and many of these estate tax returns probably impose no tax. Revenue raised from estate and gift tax in recent years comprises about 1% of federal budget receipts. This is insignificant compared to the federal individual and corporate income tax systems. Since revenue collected is minimal, the underlying rationale of the federal estate and gift tax appears to be to redistribute wealth to lower economic classes and to avoid perpetuation of an aristocratic, upper-class society.

INTRODUCTION

One can only guess at the future of the estate and gift tax laws. The Republican- controlled Congress under President George W. Bush attempted a full repeal of the estate and gift tax laws, but failed to receive the necessary 60 votes in the Senate. The vote was 54 to 44. The likely outcome, we believe, is that since death taxes have prevailed for centuries, they are likely to continue in the foreseeable future.

The purpose of this book is to provide you with a background of knowledge so that you can intelligently craft a general outline of your estate plan. If you wish, you can obtain similar background and information from an estate planning attorney and pay him or her an hourly charge for the time spent educating you on this subject. However, it is much less expensive for you to read the parts of this book that are applicable to you, gather your thoughts regarding the general outlines of an estate plan that appeals to you, and then visit an estate planning attorney. To assemble your thoughts concerning your estate plan, there are core principles that you should understand. The core principles are described in Chapter I. Subsequent chapters will describe how these core principles are utilized in developing an estate plan and specific techniques used by estate planners.

CHAPTER I

CORE PRINCIPLES

We have not segregated the core principles into tax and non-tax categories, since this will be obvious. Some important core principles are summarized below.

- <u>Unified System</u>. Under the federal tax system, the lifetime taxable gifts of the decedent and the decedent's gross estate at the time of his death are combined into a unified system under which the sum of these constitute the amount of the decedent's gross estate. The federal tax is calculated after reflecting applicable deductions and credits. Instead of calculating the taxable estate as of the date of death, if values have declined it is possible to use the "alternate valuation date," i.e. six months following the date of the decedent's death.

- <u>Estate and Gift Tax Exemption</u>. Currently, for federal estate and gift taxes, each U.S. citizen and a foreigner who is a permanent resident is entitled to a lifetime exemption of $5,340,000. This is the amount for 2014 and it is scheduled to be adjusted for inflation in subsequent years. Thus, since property passing to a surviving spouse is

CHAPTER I – CORE PRINCIPLES

deducted in calculating the taxable estate, a married couple will not be subject to federal taxes unless their combined taxable gifts and estates exceed $10,680,000. Since nothing in our tax laws is ever simple, many states also impose some form of estate or inheritance tax. The exemptions vary widely from state to state. The Illinois exemption currently is $4.0 million and is not indexed for inflation.

- Estate and Gift Tax Rates. If your combined taxable gifts and taxable estate exceed the lifetime exemption, the maximum rate of federal tax will be 40%. In addition, there is an Illinois estate tax. Illinois has enacted a complicated formula under which the Illinois estate tax is deductible. Thus, an interdependent calculation is needed to determine the Illinois tax, since the deduction is dependent on the final tax and the final tax is dependent on the deduction. Years ago it would have been necessary to tediously calculate this using a trial and error method, unless you were a mathematician who could construct a complex formula. Fortunately, during the present era, a computer will make this calculation. In order to simplify understanding of the Illinois estate tax, most planners consider the rate to be approximately 16%, but the Illinois estate tax is deductible in calculating the federal estate tax. Thus, if your estate is taxable, the combined federal and Illinois maximum rate will be approximately 50% for all amounts in excess of the applicable exemptions.

- Generation-Skipping Transfer Tax. Federal estate and gift tax incorporates a second and separate tax system, the Generation-Skipping Transfer Tax (the "GST"), that imposes a separate tax on transfers to grandchildren, great-grandchildren and trusts for their benefit. Fortunately, most of the rules and exemptions applicable to estate and gift taxes similarly apply to the GST. The GST was enacted to prevent taxpayers from transferring funds to grandchildren and lower generations, thereby bypassing the estate tax that would be payable upon the death of a child if the funds had been transferred directly to the child before being transferred a second time to a grandchild. Fortunately, most married couples will be able to avoid the GST through use of the combined $10,680,000 lifetime exemption that is applicable to the GST.

- <u>The Marital Deduction.</u>[1] Property passing to a surviving spouse is deductible and will not be subject to federal estate or Illinois estate taxes until the death of the surviving spouse, and then taxes will be incurred only if the taxable estate exceeds the lifetime exemption of the surviving spouse. To qualify for the marital deduction, it is not necessary that the surviving spouse be given the property outright. Probably in recognition of circumstances whereby most men die before their wives and men fear that a second husband will seize control of funds bequeathed outright to his wife, the estate tax laws for many years have allowed a marital deduction for funds left to a so-called "marital trust," the principal requirement of which is that the surviving spouse be given a "life estate," i.e. all of the income must be distributed annually or more frequently to the surviving spouse. This concern is equally applicable to a woman who has substantial assets and wants the funds to eventually pass to her children and not to her husband's proverbial "trophy" second wife. In order to qualify for the marital

---

[1] The marital deduction was enacted in 1948 and was intended to eliminate differences between tax treatment of couples residing in community property states and those residing in non-community property states. Until 1981, the marital deduction was limited to the greater of $250,000 or one-half of the taxpayer's adjusted gross estate. The unlimited marital deduction was enacted in 1981.

deduction, the surviving spouse must be the sole beneficiary of the marital trust, and the surviving spouse must have the right to require that all of the property of the marital trust be "income producing." The marital trust might, but need not, provide the surviving spouse with rights and powers to receive trust principal in addition to the mandatory requirement that the surviving spouse be given a "life estate" and receive all of the income.

- Unlimited Marital Deduction. The so-called "unlimited marital deduction" became part of the law in 1981, during the presidency of Ronald Reagan. Prior to that time, the marital deduction was limited to one-half of the adjusted gross estate, and the lifetime estate tax exemption was a mere $60,000 until 1976. Because of this low threshold, many people of modest means paid estate tax on the death of the first spouse to die. With proper planning, under current law there should be no estate tax until the second spouse dies, no matter how much money a married couple might have. The unlimited marital deduction dramatically changed estate planning.

- Marital Trusts. There are two common types of marital trusts.

The first is a "general power of appointment" trust that gives the surviving spouse, at the time of his or her death, the power to appoint the balance of the trust to anyone, including the estate and creditors of the surviving spouse. Typically, a general power of appointment trust provides that if the spouse fails to exercise his or her power of appointment the trust passes to the then living descendants, per stirpes. "Per stirpes" is a shorthand term of Latin derivation developed many years ago by the British that means that the children of a deceased child divide the share that the deceased child would have received if the deceased child were living. Even if you do not like words that are not plain English, accept "<u>per stirpes</u>" as language that is understood and accepted by all estate planners. This illustrates how the British lawyers, who originated this expression, have the ability to write concisely, in contrast to most American lawyers.

The second common form of marital trust is a "QTIP" trust. "QTIP" means a Qualified Terminable Interest Property. The QTIP trust provides the surviving spouse with a life estate and, for most couples in their first marriage, a limited power of appointment, e.g. a power to appoint the balance of the QTIP trust among a limited class, such as descendants. Or, as is the case in many second marriages, a QTIP trust often does not give the surviving spouse any rights or power to designate how principal will pass following his or her death. A QTIP trust customarily is used in second marriages and is designed to pass the principal of the trust to the children of the first marriage upon the death of the second spouse.

- <u>Annual Exclusion</u>. In addition to the $5,340,000 ($10,680,000 for a married couple) lifetime exemption previously discussed, each individual donor can gift up to $14,000 annually to any one or more donees without any reduction of the lifetime exemption. This is the amount for 2014, and is scheduled to be adjusted for inflation in future years. Further, a donor can pay medical and educational expenses for one or more donees (e.g. children, grandchildren and others) without any reduction of the lifetime exemption. In order to qualify for the exclusion, medical and educational expenses must be paid directly to the institution by the donor and should not be paid by a check to the donee, even though the donee sends his or her check to the institution. For larger estates where it is likely that estate tax will be incurred, full use of the annual exclusion is the most commonly used method of transferring property to descendants without payment of taxes. Since Illinois and many other states do not include gifts in determining a taxable estate, annual exclusion gifts escape both federal and Illinois taxes. Irrespective of whether an estate tax is likely to be incurred, annual exclusion gifts to children and grandchildren also can result in income tax savings by diverting income to lower bracket taxpayers.

- <u>Cost Basis of Property for Income Tax Purposes</u>. Property transferred by gift or at death may eventually be sold, whereupon income tax may be due depending on the cost basis of the property transferred. If the property passed to the recipient upon the death of a decedent and was part of the taxable estate of the decedent, the cost basis is the fair market value at the date of the decedent's death (or alternate valuation date) whether or not estate tax was incurred. This is generally referred to as obtaining a "stepped-up basis". Therefore, upon the death of the first spouse to die, despite the fact that the marital deduction eliminated payment of estate tax, the surviving spouse will receive a stepped-up basis on all assets passing to the surviving spouse from the estate of the first to die. Conversely, if property is received as a gift and is not part of the taxable estate of the donor, the donee (recipient) takes the donor's cost as the tax basis, even if the property has appreciated in value as of the date of the gift. This is commonly referred to as a "carryover basis." Upon the sale of "carryover basis" property, the recipient is subject to income taxes, often at capital gains rates, on the appreciation that occurred prior to the gift of the transferred property. Exceptions to the "carryover basis" rule are (i) for purposes of determining a loss on a future sale, the donee must use as his basis the fair market value as of the date of the gift if the property declined in value

CHAPTER I – CORE PRINCIPLES

while owned by the donor, and (ii) the donee's basis is increased by any gift taxes paid on the gift.

- <u>Portability of the Lifetime Exemption</u>. Prior to 2011, estate planners were concerned about how spouses held title to their assets since they did not want to forfeit any part of the lifetime exemption. For example, under the old law if a married couple owned property valued at $20 million, but the wife only owned $1.0 million of that property, the wife's lifetime exemption in excess of $1.0 million would be lost if she died first.

  In 2010, the law changed for decedents dying and gifts made in 2011 and thereafter. The unused portion of the deceased spouse's lifetime exemption amount ($5,340,000 in 2014) is now portable and usable by the surviving spouse. To qualify for this portability, it is necessary to timely file an estate tax return for the spouse that died first even if no estate tax return filing would otherwise be necessary. The portability provisions do not apply to the GST or to the Illinois estate tax. Thus, in instances where those taxes are likely to apply it still is necessary to carefully consider the amount of property titled in the name of each spouse in order to fully utilize both of the lifetime exemptions irrespective of who dies first.

  As you might expect, there are some very complicated and interesting rules and limitations that apply to portability of the lifetime exemption. If a surviving spouse (e.g., the "Wife") with a portable lifetime exemption from her first husband remarries and the second husband dies and leaves the Wife a second portable lifetime exemption, the applicable regulations provide that the portable lifetime exemption of the Wife is limited to the unused portable amount from the second husband. However, if the second husband outlives the Wife, the second husband can utilize the portable lifetime exemption of the Wife plus that of her first husband, but not in excess of $5,340,000. This might present an interesting subject that the Wife and the second husband may want to address in their Ante-Nuptial Agreement, i.e. how to compensate the children of the Wife's first marriage for the possible benefit to the estate of the second husband from his utilization of the portable lifetime exemption of the Wife and her first husband.

- <u>The Crummey Power</u>. From time to time in this book we will refer to a Crummey power, which was named after the taxpayer who triumphed over the IRS in a 1968 court decision. The Crummey power is a popular device commonly used in drafting trusts that gives a beneficiary of a trust the right to withdraw a portion of the annual addition to the trust corpus. This withdrawal right is usually limited to the gift tax annual exclusion (presently $14,000) and can be exercised during a limited period of time, usually within 30 days following the contribution to the trust. The Crummey power, i.e., the right to withdraw $14,000, is rarely used by the beneficiary. Instead, the $14,000 usually remains in the trust for future distribution. Typically, the beneficiary will sign a written waiver of his or her right to withdraw. The net result is that the $14,000 contributed to the trust by the donor qualifies for the gift tax annual exclusion, even though this amount remains in the trust for future distribution. The annual gift tax exclusion ordinarily does not apply to gifts of future interests, but since the Crummey power gives the beneficiary an unrestricted right to withdraw this amount, the gift to the trust is considered a present interest—not a future interest. It is even possible to broaden the scope of the $14,000 annual exclusion per donee by giving Crummey powers to a wide assortment of individuals, e.g. siblings, nieces and nephews. If a Crummey waiver is

CHAPTER I – CORE PRINCIPLES

executed by these beneficiaries, these funds will remain in the trust, and in the future may be distributed to your children if the trust so provides.

- <u>Avoidance of Probate</u>. Occasionally, but rarely, we encounter an attorney who advocates that a decedent's property pass through a probate estate, which means that there is a legal proceeding in the local probate court that appoints an executor to administer the estate. The executor identifies and collects the assets, identifies and pays the liabilities, confirms that all taxes are paid, and calculates and makes distributions to the beneficiaries, all in accordance with the provisions of the decedent's will. All of these are reflected in documents that are filed with the probate court. The only benefit of a probate proceeding, in our view, is that any creditor who does not timely file a claim in the probate proceeding is barred by a statute of limitations that is shorter than the statute of limitations that applies if no probate is filed. The disadvantages are: (a) the additional expense incurred by these filings with the probate court, (b) public disclosure in the court filings of the assets and liabilities of the decedent and the dispositions he made, and (c) perhaps most importantly, the delay involved in transferring funds to the designated transferee for investment. A probate proceeding, if done efficiently, usually takes one to two years. All of this can be done more rapidly and inexpensively without a probate proceeding.

In order to avoid probate it is important that the decedent not hold assets in his name as an individual. The most common methods of avoiding probate are: (i) decedent creates a revocable trust and transfers his assets to the revocable trust so that upon his death the successor trustee takes over without any probate proceeding; (ii) decedent holds assets in joint tenancy with another person (or tenancy by the entirety with the spouse) so that title automatically passes to the survivor; and (iii) decedent's property passes to a designated beneficiary which is the case for insurance policies, Individual Retirement Accounts and pension and profit sharing plans.

Now, with the background of the core principles described above, you are prepared to address specific estate planning options and techniques that might be applicable to you.

CHAPTER II

PLANNING FOR ESTATES UNDER THE EXEMPTION AMOUNT (CURRENTLY $10,680,000)

With a variety of exceptions, estate planning for estates that are not likely to exceed $10.7 million[2] is similar to what is done for estates that will be in excess of $10.7 million.

Gathering Factual Information

The beginning of the process is the same for estates above or below the $10.7 million exemption amount. First, the estate planner should make a factual analysis of the testator's family, identifying the individuals (or charities) who are, in a gracious old phrase, the "objects of the testator's bounty." Names and dates of birth should be collected. For the individual, spouse, children and grandchildren and their spouses, identify specific medical

---

[2] For convenience, the $10,680,000 lifetime exemption is referred to as "$10.7 million," and this represents the amount available to a married couple. The individual lifetime exemption is $5,340,000 in 2014 and will be adjusted for inflation thereafter.

CHAPTER II – PLANNING FOR ESTATES UNDER EXEMPTION AMOUNT

conditions, mental incompetency, ability or lack of ability to manage money, and their net worth and financial prospects. Also, identify any special financial needs of these individuals.

Next, the estate planner should obtain detailed information with respect to the testator's assets and liabilities. How title is held is important. Is it held in the name of the husband, wife, jointly or in trust? Make sure that life insurance and retirement accounts, including the applicable beneficiary designation forms, are given to your estate planner.

You can and should prepare and set forth this information in writing even before you meet with your estate planner. When you set up your appointment, you should ask whether he or she can send you a questionnaire or form that you can use. Doing this will make your meeting more productive than if, in the meeting, you are searching your recollections as to how title to assets is held and the names and birth dates of children and grandchildren.

Next, reflect on your objectives. For most, this is easy. Most people want to make sure that a spouse has adequate funds for the remainder of his or her life, and then want the balance to pass to their children. But there are many variations. What if you are in a second marriage with children from a first marriage? What if you have no children or if your children die while your spouse is still living? Some individuals want to make provision for their parents, siblings and/or charities.

The Typical and Usual Structure of Estate Planning Documents

The typical structure of estate planning documents for estates under $10.7 million is similar to those for estates over $10.7 million. It is important that you know the structure that is customary. You might decide to modify, but it usually is better to start with an existing model than to try to craft a new and original model.

CHAPTER II – PLANNING FOR ESTATES UNDER EXEMPTION AMOUNT

The typical or usual estate plan usually involves the following documents:

1. <u>Will and Guardianship</u>. A so-called "Pour Over Will" that leaves any property that remains in your name to a revocable trust previously created by you. The Pour Over Will should designate an executor and successors who will collect the assets held in your name, handle the probate proceedings, if there are any (hopefully there will be no probate proceedings), file necessary estate and income tax returns, pay your outstanding debts, pay administration expenses of the estate, and distribute the balance to the revocable trust, i.e. the balance of the estate pours over into the revocable trust.

If there are minor children, the Will or a "side letter" frequently designates guardians for the minor children. Often the selection of a guardian to raise the minor children following the death of both spouses is a very difficult decision that is filled with anxieties. A guardian must be appointed by the court, and the parent's designation does not bind the court, although it usually will be followed by the court absent a contest and good reason to depart from the direction of the parents. Our advice usually is to make the best choice that you can make at that time and review the choice frequently since your views regarding the designation of a guardian are likely to change with greater frequency than your views regarding disposition of property. For that reason, we recommend a "side letter" for designating a guardian rather than doing this in your Will.

2. <u>Revocable Trust for Estates in Excess of $10.7 Million</u>. This document will be the foundation of your estate plan. It will set forth the beneficiaries and the pattern of distributions. Although this Chapter II is entitled "Planning for Estates Under the Exemption Amount (Currently $10,680,000)," the terms of the Revocable Trust for those estates are so similar to terms used for

CHAPTER II – PLANNING FOR ESTATES UNDER EXEMPTION AMOUNT

estates over $10.7 million that we felt it appropriate to consider both types of Revocable Trusts in this Chapter II. We first will consider the terms of a Revocable Trust used by most married couples with estates that exceed $10.7 million. Below is the typical pattern for distribution:

(a) The document generally creates two trusts. A marital trust is funded with the amount, if any, that is in excess of the lifetime estate tax exemption (presently $5,340,000). The nonmarital trust will be funded with the amount of the lifetime exemption (presently $5,340,000) reduced by the total of taxable gifts made during the decedent's lifetime, or a lesser amount if the decedent's assets are less than $5,340,000.

(b) Generally, the terms of the marital trust and the nonmarital trust are the same: (i) pay all income annually or more frequently to the surviving spouse, (ii) the trustee has discretion to pay principal to the surviving spouse for his or her health, support and maintenance, and (iii) upon the death of the surviving spouse the trust passes to the descendants, per stirpes, if the trust is a QTIP trust. If the martial trust is a general power of appointment trust, the surviving spouse can appoint the trust in any manner he or she designates. If the trust is a QTIP trust that has a limited power of appointment, the balance will pass to those descendants designated by the surviving spouse, or if the power of appointment is not exercised, the trust will pass to the descendants, per stirpes.

(c) After both spouses die, if their trusts continue for their children, the marital and nonmarital trusts usually are combined and a new trust is created for each child, specifying that funds payable to a child under age 21, or in some cases age 25, will remain in the trust until he or she attains a specified age for distribution of the principal. Typically, the principal of the children's trusts are distributed at three 5-year intervals, such as one-third at age 40, one-half of the balance at age 45 and the

CHAPTER II – PLANNING FOR ESTATES UNDER EXEMPTION AMOUNT

balance at age 50, but parents often will create so-called "dynasty trusts" that extend beyond the lifetime of their children.

(d) In our experience, the most perplexing question to clients is who should be named as trustee and successors. Should it be a bank, one or more individuals, or a combination? This decision must be made by you. Banks are very competent, provide quality trust administration services, have vast experience in investing in securities, but they charge annual fees of approximately 1% - 1.5% for trusts under $10 million. You might be fortunate to have a family member or a trusted advisor that you want to designate as trustee. If a bank is designated as the trustee, often there is a provision giving the beneficiaries the right to remove the bank and appoint another bank as trustee. This provision is intended to assure that the initial bank trustee will carefully and diligently service this trust and its beneficiaries, or else risk removal if the beneficiaries are disappointed by the bank's performance. Using a bank as a trustee or co-trustee can assure that the assets will be protected throughout the life and following the death of the surviving spouse. There have been many horror stories of the waste and loss of assets that were left (outright or in a trust) under the control of a gullible or naïve spouse or children lacking the experience and independence offered by a bank serving as trustee.

(e) A variety of provisions can be inserted into the marital trust to provide the surviving spouse with greater ability to have immediate access to these funds. For example, the surviving spouse can be given the power to withdraw all or any part of the marital trust upon request. A more limited provision might be to give the surviving spouse the right to withdraw a specified amount of principal each year in addition to receiving all of the income. For the marital trust, the trustee frequently is given the discretion to distribute principal to the surviving spouse for his or her "best interests." Since the marital trust will be includable in the taxable estate of the surviving spouse upon the

CHAPTER II – PLANNING FOR ESTATES UNDER EXEMPTION AMOUNT

death of the surviving spouse, a variety of personally preferred provisions can be used since these will not affect the tax results on the death of the surviving spouse. However, it is essential to exercise great caution to assure that the surviving spouse is the only beneficiary of the marital trust, is entitled to receive all of the income annually or more frequently, and is entitled to require that investments be in income-producing assets.

(f) For the nonmarital trust, it is important to avoid provisions that will cause the nonmarital trust to be included in the taxable estate of the surviving spouse upon the death of the surviving spouse, e.g., do not give the surviving spouse the right to withdraw principal or a general power of appointment.

3. <u>Revocable Trust for Estates Under $10.7 Million</u>. Until several years ago, when the lifetime estate tax exemption was about $2.0 million for a married couple and the maximum federal income tax rates were 15% on long-term capital gains and 37.5% on ordinary income, the terms of revocable trusts were about the same, irrespective of the size of the married couple's taxable estate. In the old days of 2001, when the estate tax lifetime exemption was $675,000 for an individual, the focus of estate planning was to remove assets from the taxable estate. But now that the estate tax exemption has increased to $10.7 million for a married couple and the maximum federal income tax rates have increased to 23.8% for long-term capital gains and 44% for ordinary income (both of these without including state income taxes), a new strategy has developed in drafting revocable trusts for married couples whose wealth is not likely to ever exceed the $10.7 million threshold. Since no estate tax is likely, the new primary objective is to minimize income taxes by achieving a step-up in basis to the value of assets at the time of the death of the second-to-die of the married couple. No longer is the income tax basis of assets a secondary consideration since the increased lifetime exemption will protect many couples from incurring any estate taxes.

CHAPTER II – PLANNING FOR ESTATES UNDER EXEMPTION AMOUNT

Thus, instead of planning to bypass the taxable estate of the second-to-die, the parties may choose the opposite objective, namely, to make sure that the assets of the first-to-die of the spouses will be included in the taxable estate of the surviving spouse. This will be the case if everyone is confident there will not be any estate tax due by reason of the increased lifetime exemption. The basis of assets will then be stepped-up to the value at the time of the death of the second-to-die. Upon the subsequent sale of these assets, the appreciation that occurred during the period following the death of the first spouse to the time of the death of the second spouse will escape being subject to any ordinary income or capital gains tax.

The technique for achieving this step-up in basis is a simple change in the language of the revocable trust that will fund the marital trust first, instead of first funding the nonmarital trust, and also provide the trustees of the marital trust, following the decedent's death, the right to disclaim and pass the disclaimed funds to the nonmarital trust. Since a qualified disclaimer must be done within nine months following the death of the first-to-die, the surviving spouse and advisors can consider and determine the wisest course. They must take into account the age of the surviving spouse and whether the assets of the decedent are likely to significantly appreciate during the lifetime of the surviving spouse. They can elect to retain assets in the Marital Trust so that the basis of these assets will be stepped-up to the value at the time of the death of the surviving spouse. Alternatively, they can disclaim so that these assets will not be included in the taxable estate of the surviving spouse, but the effect of the disclaimer is that the assets will, for income tax purposes, retain a basis equal to the value at the date of death of the first-to-die of the spouses.

4. <u>Health Care Power of Attorney</u>. This document designates the individual to act as your agent. Usually this is a spouse or a child who is authorized to make health care decisions for you if you are not capable of making these yourself. In the Health Care Power of Attorney form, you should specify your

CHAPTER II – PLANNING FOR ESTATES UNDER EXEMPTION AMOUNT

wishes concerning life support and other medical decisions. If there is a question to "pull the plug" or keep you on a life support system, your health care agent will make the decision. Do not believe that this form was intended to carry out your wishes, although it is likely to do so. The document was intended to protect doctors and hospitals, and authorizes them to follow the directions of your designated health care agent. There should not be two people who jointly act in this capacity. Only one person should act as your health care agent, but there can be successors named in case the initially designated person is not available to act. Do not rely solely on the Health Care Power of Attorney. Discuss this subject with your spouse and children to make sure they understand and will abide by your wishes. Make sure they have in their possession an original of the latest version of your Health Care Power of Attorney, since this is likely to be called for at a time when you do not have the capacity to find it. Most doctors and hospitals will accept a copy and not require the original. The Health Care Power of Attorney should be kept where it is accessible to your agent. We recommend against placing this in a safe deposit box that might not be accessible in the event of an emergency.

5. <u>Property Power of Attorney</u>. This document designates an individual to act as your agent in making financial and other decisions for you if you are not capable of making these yourself. Hopefully, you will accomplish the transfer of title to all of your assets into your revocable trust before you become incapacitated or terminally ill, and if that is the case, the scope of this document is limited, since the trustee of your revocable trust is empowered to make the important financial decisions. Nevertheless, there are occasions when a Property Power of Attorney will be necessary to transfer title to property or provide for payments from governmental agencies (e.g. Social Security and Medicare). In current times with an aging population, instances of incapacity are much more prevalent, and a Property Power of Attorney is an important estate planning document.

CHAPTER II – PLANNING FOR ESTATES UNDER EXEMPTION AMOUNT

Disposition of Assets through Joint Tenancies and Beneficiary Designations

It is a rare case, but possible, for an individual to be able to pass all of his or her assets without having a Will or a revocable trust. This can be done by using a combination of (i) beneficiary designations for life insurance policies and retirement accounts, (ii) joint tenancies (or tenancy by entirety with a surviving spouse), and (iii) bank and investment accounts that transfer to a designated beneficiary. You might find the simplicity of this plan to be attractive. But bear in mind that, unless you designate a trust as the beneficiary of life insurance and retirement accounts, these will likely pass to your spouse outright. For a tenancy by the entirety with your spouse, the subject asset (in Illinois, only a primary residence) automatically passes to him or her upon your death. Therefore, although the plan sounds simple, the funds passing outright to your spouse will be vulnerable to being spent by a second husband or a second trophy wife and might never be passed on to your children as you intended. In addition, this simple plan exposes assets to creditors of your beneficiaries or to unwarranted, extravagant spending by the beneficiaries. This can be prevented by leaving the assets in trust for the benefit of the beneficiaries.

If the taxable estate of a married couple does not and will not exceed $10.7 million (or $8.0 million for Illinois residents), or one-half of these amounts if you are not married, you might want to discontinue reading this book and merely skim the remainder to see if any of the subjects covered are of interest to you. The balance of this book will discuss the valuation of assets and some of the commonly used techniques for reducing your taxable estate if you believe it will exceed $10.7 million.

CHAPTER III

VALUATION

To the extent that your assets consist of marketable securities, certificates of deposit, savings accounts, money market funds or similar items, valuation is not a problem. But what is the value of other assets – closely-held business interests, real estate, valuable pieces of art, etc. – when you die or make a gift of these items to your family? There are knowledgeable appraisers and other experts that can provide values. When you are transferring assets that are difficult to value, we recommend that you obtain a valuation from a qualified appraiser or expert in the form of a written report setting forth the value and the support for his or her determination of value.

Obviously, in most cases where the estate will exceed the $10.7 million threshold, the taxpayer wants to obtain the lowest possible valuation, and the Internal Revenue Service ("IRS") will want the highest possible valuation.[3] In our experience, most of

---

[3] In situations where the estate is not subject to estate taxes, it usually is beneficial to the taxpayer to establish a high value and step up the basis to that value, thereby minimizing the income taxes on a subsequent sale of the asset. Failing to obtain valuation is likely to result in you, your accountant or the IRS assuming a lower value, thereby increasing your income taxes.

CHAPTER III - VALUATION

the estate and gift tax disputes with the IRS are over a difference of opinion regarding valuation of a particular asset that is difficult to value.

If you think you can successfully slide a low valuation past the IRS, think again! The IRS has engineering departments, appraisers and experts that are very good. They can spot a low valuation and know how to come up with a high valuation. Think of the IRS the same way you thought of the strongest and toughest kid in your neighborhood when you were a youth. Unless you were crazy or dumb, you would not challenge him to a fight. Good advice is, whenever possible, avoid a fight with someone stronger and tougher.

Although the IRS is formidable in a valuation dispute, the IRS is handicapped by the fact that the valuation issues they encounter are those reflected on filed gift tax returns or estate tax returns.. Therefore, utilize the IRS's handicap to your advantage just as you avoided fighting a stronger and tougher kid. If you are trying to transfer to your family assets that are difficult to value, do so during your lifetime utilizing the annual exclusions so that these assets are never reflected on any gift or estate tax return. If a difficult-to-value asset does not appear on your gift or estate tax return, it is likely to escape the attention of the IRS. Thus, we recommend making the transfer by a gift or series of gifts that are within the annual exclusions and need not be reported, a sale of the asset to a family member (see below), or creating a partnership or other entity with family members in which you contribute the difficult-to-value asset and they contribute cash or other property.

Many estate planners will disagree with our last sentence and advise that you should make the transfer and report it on a gift tax return in order to start the running of the 3-year statute of limitations. There might be some validity to this if the gift tax return reflects that the value of the gift will not come close to

CHAPTER III - VALUATION

exhausting your remaining $5,340,000 unused lifetime exemption. Although we see some validity to the argument for filing a gift tax return, we generally follow the pattern of avoiding fighting the stronger and tougher kid by minimizing contacts with him. A valuation fight with the IRS is difficult and very expensive. It usually can be avoided if the IRS is not presented with a gift or estate tax return that reflects a difficult-to-value asset.

Our ultimate objective is to transfer all difficult-to-value assets during the taxpayer's lifetime, without gift tax reporting, so that the estate tax return only reflects cash and marketable securities. There is little incentive for the IRS to audit an estate tax return if it only reflects cash and marketable securities.

Another technique used to avoid a valuation dispute with the IRS is to sell the difficult-to-value asset to family members at a price equal to the appraised value or a price that you are confident is equal to fair market value. If the family members do not have sufficient cash to make the purchase, give them a gift of cash to pay you the purchase price or take a promissory note in exchange for the asset and periodically gift the sums due under the note. A gift of cash or a promissory note, even if reported on a gift tax return, is not likely to create a valuation dispute.

Bear in mind that we do not recommend proceeding with these gift or sale techniques without an appraisal. In the event the IRS audits you in the future, you need to know your values in order to justify not reporting a gift. If you gift or sell an asset for $10,000 that is later proven to be worth $50,000, you have a $40,000 unreported gift, which could lead to taxes, penalties and interest.

Also, you can avoid valuation disputes with the IRS by leaving the difficult-to-value asset to a charity. By doing so, the value is irrelevant since an increase in value results in a corresponding

CHAPTER III - VALUATION

increase in the charitable deduction. This is the customary method used to dispose of a valuable art collection.

Chapter IV will consider in greater detail what we regard as the "Grand Slam", i.e. the best available technique for transferring wealth to your family – a sale of a difficult-to-value asset that produces large amounts of taxable income to a defective trust.

CHAPTER IV

THE GRAND SLAM: SALE TO A DEFECTIVE TRUST

Chapter IV – The Grand Slam: Sale to a Defective Trust

Although practitioners and the IRS are well aware of the substantial tax savings accomplished through the sale of assets to a defective trust, this technique remains available, but it is questionable whether it will continue to survive. In 2013, the Obama administration's budget proposal recommended a statutory change that would terminate this tax saving device in 2014, but as of the time of this writing this proposal has not been enacted. We advise that this strategy be implemented as soon as possible since how much longer this strategy will be available is unknown.

The defective trust, sometimes called a grantor trust, is a trust that is treated one way for income tax purposes and a totally different way for estate and gift tax purposes. Qualification as a defective trust is simple. It involves adding one or more meaningless provisions to the trust agreement, e.g. a power permitting the grantor (i.e. the individual creating the defective

CHAPTER IV – THE GRAND SLAM: SALE TO A DEFECTIVE TRUST

trust) to add beneficiaries, a power permitting the grantor to borrow without adequate interest and adequate security, or a power permitting the grantor to substitute assets of an equivalent value. If a trust is defective, for income tax purposes the trust is ignored and the trust income is taxed to the grantor. Also, if the grantor sells appreciated assets to the defective trust, the sale is disregarded and it is treated as if the grantor was dealing with himself and merely shifted the asset from one of his pockets to the other pocket.

But for gift and estate tax purposes, the defective trust is not disregarded and is treated as a legitimate trust. If funds are gifted to the defective trust, this is regarded as a legitimate gift and the funds are not included in the grantor's taxable estate. Only in the complexities of the U.S. tax system could such a ridiculous and illogical result be achieved.

This tax loophole, which has opened a wonderful estate planning opportunity, was created in 1954 when Congress passed an income tax statute that thwarted high-bracket income taxpayers from shifting income to low-bracket trusts, even though the grantor controlled the trust. We doubt that Congress was aware of the estate tax loophole it created. Estate planners now prepare an intentionally defective trust so that the grantor pays all of the income tax on trust income despite the fact that the trust income will pass to the grantor's heirs without being subject to gift or estate tax. In considering this, it is necessary to balance the tax benefits against the possibility that the grantor's income might be subject to higher bracket income tax rates than those applicable to his beneficiaries.

We illustrate this with an example of a typical transaction. A very wealthy individual (the "Grandfather") owns all of the outstanding stock of ABC Corporation, an S Corporation, that generates $6.0 million of pre-tax annual income that will be distributed annually to shareholders. Grandfather obtains an

CHAPTER IV – THE GRAND SLAM: SALE TO A DEFECTIVE TRUST

appraisal of ABC of $30 million before discounts for lack of marketability and minority interests. The beneficiaries of the defective trust are his four children, their spouses, and twelve grandchildren, i.e. a total of twenty beneficiaries. The defective trust has Crummey powers (see page 11 of this book) permitting use of $560,000 (20 x $14,000 x 2) of gift tax exclusions each year by Grandfather and his spouse ("Grandmother"). On December 31st, Grandfather and Grandmother each gift $280,000 (a total of $560,000) of cash to the defective trust and they repeat those gifts on January 1st. Thus, on January 2nd the defective trust has $1,120,000 of cash ($560,000 x 2). It might be advisable to make an additional taxable cash gift of $630,000 to the defective trust to increase its principal amount of $1,750,000 that is equal to approximately 10% of the $17,550,000 purchase price described in the following paragraph. The taxable gift of $630,000 will not result in an immediate tax if it is within the $5,340,000 lifetime exemption available to each of Grandfather and Grandmother.

Using a 35% overall discount[4] to the $30 million valuation of ABC Corporation, Grandfather sells 90% of non-voting ABC stock to the defective trust for $17,550,000 ($30,000,000 x 65% x 90%), payable $1.0 million in cash at closing and a $16,550,000 promissory note payable over nine years, together with interest determined under the current Applicable Federal Rate ("AFR") of 1.82%. No capital gains tax will be incurred on the sale since Grandfather is treated as selling the stock to himself. Over the next six years, the defective trust that owns 90% of ABC Corporation will receive $32,400,000 ($6.0 million x 6 x 90%) of income, but will not pay any income taxes since Grandfather will be responsible for these income taxes. Thus, in a 6-year period, the trust can pay off the $16,550,000 debt. After six years the trust will own 90% of the ABC stock and will have $16,600,000 of

---

[4] See Chapter V for explanation of the discounts commonly used by appraisers in valuing minority or non-voting interests in closely-held corporations.

CHAPTER IV – THE GRAND SLAM: SALE TO A DEFECTIVE TRUST

cash[5], without reflecting any income or appreciation realized on the investment of available cash, and without those assets ever being subject to gift or estate taxes. Moreover, the taxable estate of Grandfather has been depleted by the payment of more than $13.0 million of income taxes on $32,400,000 of taxable income that will pass to his heirs. By retaining the voting stock of ABC Corporation, Grandfather has had voting control throughout this entire period.

Another potential benefit is the possibility that the ABC stock purchased by the defective trust will appreciate in value during the term of the defective trust.

The drawbacks are negligible compared to the potential benefits. If ABC fails to generate sufficient cash to pay the debt of the defective trust, the trust can make payment by giving back a portion of the ABC stock without any adverse income tax consequences. Another drawback is that the beneficiaries do not get a stepped-up basis for their ABC stock since the stock was never subject to estate tax. If the grantor, over the years, finds that his cash flow is impaired by paying income taxes on income that will pass to his beneficiaries, this can be addressed in the defective trust by including a provision that allows a termination of grantor trust treatment and results in imposing on the trust or its beneficiaries the liability for income taxes applicable to income earned after the termination.

There are a multitude of variations to the use of intentionally defective trusts that will change depending on the particular facts, but this probably is the best of all of the present estate planning

---

[5] Cash from original gifts ($1,120,000 + $630,000) $ 1,750,000
Income received over 6-yr. period from ABC   32,400,000
Less cash payments to Grandfather for
  purchase of ABC stock (excluding interest)   <17,550,000>
Total cash held by defective trust: $16,600,000

CHAPTER IV – THE GRAND SLAM: SALE TO A DEFECTIVE TRUST

techniques for reducing estate taxes. Hopefully, Congress will not legislate the end to this phenomenal tax loophole.

CHAPTER V

FAMILY LIMITED PARTNERSHIPS

Although we are using the term Family Limited Partnership ("FLP") for the tax savings procedures described in this chapter, these procedures also apply to business entities other than a limited partnership, e.g., a corporation (particularly an S corporation that is taxed similar to a partnership), a limited liability company ("LLC") or a general partnership. This chapter will consider how to transfer business entities and investment entities, each of which we will refer to as an FLP from the older generation to younger generations.

The typical goals of the older generation are:

1. Transfer wealth to the younger generations incurring only the minimum amount of overall income, estate and gift tax.

2. Retain control of the FLP.

A number of techniques are available to accomplish these objectives. The FLP became a popular form of planning lifetime

CHAPTER V – FAMILY LIMITED PARTNERSHIPS

giving due to various court decisions that upheld the position that there can be significant discounts in calculating the value of the transferred interests in the FLP. In valuing FLP interests being transferred, there is a substantial discount for "lack of marketability" that is intended to reflect the difference between value of publicly-traded companies and those that are privately held. The other generally accepted discount is the one given for lack of control, often referred to as a "minority interest discount." Although the amounts attributed to these discounts may vary greatly depending on the appraiser, it is common for the aggregate of these discounts to be approximately 30% to 40% of the total value. Thus, in lieu of transferring an asset, such as a parcel of real estate, directly to a donee, the real estate or other asset can be transferred to an FLP, and a fractional interest can then be gifted using a discounted value of 60% to 70% of the appraised value.

If the FLP is a so-called "investment company" where more than 80% of the value of its assets are held for investment and consist of cash, stocks and securities, certain limitations apply. A business purpose should exist for the forming of the FLP, but usually the objective of involving the younger generation in management will be regarded as a valid business purpose. If each of the owners of the FLP transfer different stocks or securities to a newly-formed FLP, the IRS may attempt to impose a tax under the rationale that the taxpayer has diversified his portfolio and, therefore, the appreciation should be subject to income taxes. Another limitation applicable to "investment companies" is that the discount allowable for non-marketability and minority interest usually is in the range of 10% to 15% of the underlying asset value, as compared to a 30% to 40% range for an FLP that owns and operates a business.

As stated earlier, an FLP can own an ongoing business entity, real estate or publicly-traded stocks and bonds. The older generation, e.g. Grandfather, may already own assets in an FLP or

CHAPTER V – FAMILY LIMITED PARTNERSHIPS

may transfer assets to a newly-created limited partnership, LLC or S corporation that becomes the FLP. Assuming Grandfather owns 100% of the FLP, the FLP can be recapitalized into voting and non-voting interests. It is not uncommon to find that 99% of the equity and income of the FLP is assigned to the non-voting interests. Grandfather obtains a very favorable appraisal of the non-voting interests from a clever independent appraiser who uses creative but customary, established principles, first to reduce the overall value of the FLP and second to finalize a very low value for the non-voting interests in the FLP by applying a 30%-40% discount.[6]

Grandfather is now in a position to significantly reduce his taxable estate without diminishing his control of the FLP. A number of paths are possible. Grandfather can gift the non-voting interests in the FLP among his children, grandchildren, their spouses and trusts for their benefit. Assuming Grandfather is married, he and his wife can gift $28,000 per year to each donee under the gift tax annual exclusion. If Grandfather gifts $14,000 of non-voting interests per donee to his wife and she subsequently gifts this to donees in the younger generation, no gift tax return is required. The IRS will probably never learn of the gift or the appraisal of the FLP non-voting interests.

If the $28,000 annual gifts are not sufficient to accomplish the desired reduction of Grandfather's taxable estate, Grandfather and his wife can gift non-voting interests in the FLP utilizing their combined $10.7 million lifetime exemption. Thereafter, all of the income from and appreciation in value of the transferred non-voting FLP interests will accrue to the younger

---

[6] In valuing an interest in an FLP, appraisers usually take a "marketability discount" because the interest is not marketable and a second "minority interest discount" because the interest is non-voting or not the controlling interest. Typically, the sum of these discounts is between 30%-40%.

generations without being subject to estate taxes when Grandfather and Grandmother die.

If this still is not sufficient to accomplish the desired reduction of Grandfather's taxable estate, Grandfather can sell non-voting interests in the FLP to the younger generation at the favorable appraised value, but this might result in a capital gain to Grandfather. The capital gain problem can be avoided by the creation of a defective trust and the sale of the non-voting FLP interests to the defective trust, as described in Chapter IV. Not only will this result in excluding from Grandfather's taxable estate all of the subsequent income and growth in value over the appraised value of the transferred non-voting FLP interests, but, in addition, Grandfather will reduce his taxable estate by paying the income tax applicable to the income of the transferred non-voting FLP interests.

After accomplishing the reductions described above, if the resulting estate tax on the taxable estate of Grandfather and Grandmother still is at an unacceptably high level, read the subsequent chapters, particularly Chapter VI relating to the charitable deduction, to see how the super-rich avoid payment of excessive federal estate taxes.

Chapter VI

THE CHARITABLE DEDUCTION

Use of a Private Foundation

The centerpiece estate planning technique for the super-rich is utilization of the charitable deduction. Although this became part of the estate tax law in 1918, Henry Ford and his only son, Edsel Ford, popularized the utilization of the charitable deduction to reduce federal estate taxes.

In 1908, Henry Ford began mass production of the Model T. The Ford Foundation was established in 1936 to avoid the substantial estate taxes imposed by Franklin D. Roosevelt's administration. Following the deaths of Edsel (in 1943) and Henry (in 1947), 90% of the non-voting shares of Ford Motor Company were owned by the Ford Foundation. The Ford family retained the voting shares. The Ford Foundation sold all of its Ford Motor Company holdings between 1955 and 1974, and no longer has any significant ownership in the publicly-held company that manufactures automobiles.

The example set by Henry and Edsel Ford has been widely followed. Utilizing the combination of voting and non-voting interests and a transfer to a private foundation achieves avoidance of estate tax while still maintaining control of the

CHAPTER VI – THE CHARITABLE DEDUCTION

company. A private foundation that is controlled by family members will provide these family members with esteemed positions in their communities by reason of their ability to contribute to various philanthropic causes.

A private foundation is defined in negative terms as a charity that does not receive substantial support from the general public. In addition, each of the following requirements must be met:

- It must be organized and operated exclusively for certain enumerated charitable and public purposes.

- No part of the net earnings may inure to benefit any private individual or shareholder.

- No substantial activities are to carry out propaganda or attempt to influence legislation.

- It must not participate in political activities.

Under the following sections of the Internal Revenue Code ("IRC"), there are specific taxes and operating restrictions that are applicable to private foundations:

- A 2% excise tax is imposed each year on net investment income. (§4940)

- Self-dealing between a private foundation and its donors or related parties ("disqualified persons") are prohibited and subject to excise taxes and other sanctions. (§4941)

- A private foundation is required to distribute annually an amount equal to at least 5% of the fair market value of its assets, commonly called the "minimum income distribution requirements." (§4942)

CHAPTER VI – THE CHARITABLE DEDUCTION

- To curb the use of serving as a vehicle for controlling business enterprises, there are complex rules prohibiting private foundations and disqualified persons from jointly owning excess business holdings. (§4943)

- High-risk investments (e.g. trading on margin or commodity futures; investing in "puts," "calls," "straddles" or warrants; investing in working interests in oil or gas wells; and short selling) are prohibited. (§4944)

- Certain payments by a private foundation (called "taxable expenditures") that are to influence politics, legislation or propaganda are subject to an initial 20% tax and further levels of tax exceeding 100% if not promptly corrected.

Despite these requirements and restrictions, it is relatively easy to qualify as a private foundation and successfully navigate the restrictions. It is customary to apply for and quickly obtain a "determination letter" from the IRS that the organization, usually a not-for-profit corporation, qualifies as a tax-exempt private foundation.

Private foundations pre-date enactment of laws imposing income and estate taxes. The Carnegie and the Rockefeller foundations were established about 1907. Published data confirms that in 2010 there were 120,810 private foundations in the United States with total assets just under $600 billion. Near the close of 2012, the five largest private foundations were as follows:

	Assets Exceeding
Bill & Melinda Gates Foundation	$37 billion
Ford Foundation	$11 billion
J. Paul Getty Trust	$10 billion
The Robert Wood Johnson Foundation	$ 9 billion
The William and Flora Hewlett Foundation	$ 8 billion

CHAPTER VI – THE CHARITABLE DEDUCTION

Two of these, namely, the Ford Foundation and The Robert Wood Johnson Foundation, as well as the seventh largest foundation, Lilly Endowment, Inc., with assets slightly under $7 billion, were formed in the same period of 1936-1937. We leave it to historians to determine whether this was merely coincidental or whether the founding tycoons communicated with each other before establishing what have grown into massive private foundations.

Income Tax Deduction

Gifts to charity also will provide the donor with significant income tax benefits, but the calculation of the charitable deduction depends on whether the charitable donee is a public or private charity, whether the property contributed would result in a long-term gain or ordinary income if sold, and whether the property contributed is publicly-traded stock. Below is a summary of the applicable income tax rules:

- Gifts to public charities by an individual of cash or cash equivalents, i.e. property other than long-term capital gain property or ordinary income property, are deductible by an individual up to 50% of his adjusted gross income.

- Gifts of long-term capital gain property to a public charity by an individual are deductible up to 30% of the donor's adjusted gross income.

- For ordinary income property gifted by an individual to a public charity, the deduction is reduced by the ordinary income that would have been recognized and the deduction is allowed up to 50% of the donor's adjusted gross income.

CHAPTER VI – THE CHARITABLE DEDUCTION

- Gifts to private foundations can be deducted by an individual up to a limit of 20% of the donor's adjusted gross income, and in the case of a gift of long-term gain property other than marketable securities, the deduction is reduced by the amount of the long-term gain.

In making a charitable gift, other income tax limitations need to be considered, but these are beyond the scope of this book. These include carry-forwards of deductions in excess of the deductible ceiling, election to apply the 50% deductible ceiling by reducing the contribution by the long-term capital gain, limitations applicable to gifts of intellectual property, and others.

CRATs and CRUTs

Congress has enacted legislation that authorizes a variety of charitable entities, known as "split-interest trusts." One of the popular split-interest trusts is a charitable remainder trust. This trust is required to make payments annually during the life or lives of the grantors of the trust or for a term of years, not exceeding 20 years, to one or more non-charitable beneficiaries with the remainder payable to charity. If the required payment is a sum certain, i.e. an annuity, the trust is called a "Charitable Remainder Annuity Trust," or "CRAT". If the required annual payment is the net income or a fixed percentage of the annual fair-market value, the trust is called a "Charitable Remainder Unitrust," or "CRUT".

A CRAT or a CRUT frequently is used by a taxpayer in a high income tax bracket who is approaching retirement, at which time he believes his income and tax bracket will be reduced, and has an impending sale of a long-term capital gain asset. Prior to the sale of the capital asset, the taxpayer donates the asset to the CRAT or CRUT and reserves the right to receive about 5% of its value each year for 20 years. The taxpayer can designate alternate beneficiaries to receive payment if he dies prior to the expiration of the term. The effects are as follows:

- taxpayer will receive about 100% of the value of the donated asset payable over 20 years;

- by reason of the annual distributions to the taxpayer, the long-term capital gain will be taxed annually over the 20-year period, possibly at lower rates than those that would apply if the tax were paid by the taxpayer in the year of sale;

- there is no long-term capital gains tax on the contribution of the asset to the CRAT or CRUT;

- the taxpayer will receive an income tax deduction in the year he transfers the asset to the CRAT or CRUT; and

- the corpus of the CRAT or CRUT will yield greater amounts of annual income since payments of the long-term capital gains tax is postponed and paid out of the income distributed by the CRAT or CRUT without reduction of the principal.

Depending on the earnings of the CRAT or CRUT, it is possible that, despite the payment to the donor of 100% of the proceeds of sale, the eventual distribution to the charity will equal or exceed 100% of the sales proceeds. Such a result would be highly unlikely if the long-term capital gains tax was paid in the year of sale and only about 75% of the sales proceeds remained for investment. Also, the taxpayer/donor retained for himself a significant amount of annual payments to provide him with financial security. The remainder that passes to charity is deductible in calculating the taxpayer's taxable estate.

CHAPTER VI – THE CHARITABLE DEDUCTION

The Charitable Remainder Trust is an appealing technique for the sale of a substantially appreciated asset and the reinvestment in a diversified portfolio without the immediate payment of tax on the long-term capital gain. The objective is to achieve a significant enhancement of the current income since there is no immediate capital gains tax on the proceeds of the sale.

Charitable Lead Trust

A Charitable Lead Trust ("CLT") is the opposite of a Charitable Remainder Trust. In a CLT, the charitable beneficiary begins to receive income payments immediately upon the funding of the trust, and the remainder interest usually will pass to the grantor's family on the expiration of the charity's right to receive income.

There are two distinct types of CLTs, a non-grantor CLT and a grantor CLT. The balance of this chapter will describe a non-grantor, inter vivos CLT.

The non-grantor, inter vivos CLT is best suited for taxpayers with substantial income-producing assets who can afford to forego receipt of income from certain assets for a number of years. The primary benefits of the CLT are:

1. The actuarial value of the income interest given to charity is deducted from the value of property transferred to the trust in calculating the amount of the donor's gift of the remainder interest to his family.

2. Although the donor will not receive an income tax charitable deduction upon creation of the trust, the payments to charity will be deductible in calculating the annual income of the trust and will not be subject to the percentage limitations that are applicable to an individual who creates a CRAT or CRUT.

CHAPTER VI – THE CHARITABLE DEDUCTION

The CLT was a popular technique back in the late 1980s when practitioners discovered that the value of the income interest calculated under the actuarial valuation tables that was the measure of the annual amount payable to charity was substantially lower than actual prevailing interest rates. Therefore, the non-charitable beneficiary, i.e. the family member, received the benefit of the excess of the actual income over the value of the income interest reflected in the actuarial tables. In 1989, the statute was changed and the assumed interest rate used in valuing the charitable interest generally will correspond to the actual interest rate. Thus, presently the Charitable Lead Trust is not as widely used as a Charitable Remainder Trust.

Chapter VII

LIFE INSURANCE

Life insurance originated during ancient times. History reflects that there were private dealings involving life insurance among citizens of the Roman Empire. This came into prominence in 18th century England when parties gambled on another person's mortality, which led to the Gambling Act of 1774 that prohibited the purchase of life insurance unless the policy owner had a financial interest in the insured. This requirement of a so-called "insurable interest" prevails today in England and the U.S.A.

Inclusion in Decedent's Gross Estate

Section 2042 of the Internal Revenue Code ("IRC") includes life insurance on the life of a decedent within the decedent's gross estate if (i) it is receivable by his executor, or (ii) if the decedent possessed any "incidents of ownership" in life insurance payable to beneficiaries other than the decedent's executor. The typical "incidents of ownership" that cause a policy to be included in the decedent's estate are the following powers retained by the decedent: to change the beneficiary, to surrender or cancel the policy, to assign the policy, and to obtain a loan from the insurance company or a third party using the policy as collateral. A power that rises to the level of an incident of ownership will cause the policy to be included in the decedent's gross estate if it is held by the decedent alone or if shared with another person, irrespective of whether the other person is related, subservient or adverse. A power by the decedent to consent to or veto the action of another person with respect to life insurance is a taxable power. A power held by the decedent as trustee or co-trustee is an incident of ownership despite the existence of a fiduciary obligation.

If a decedent makes a gift of a life insurance policy on his life within a three-year period prior to his death, the proceeds of the policy are includable in the decedent's gross estate under Section 2035 of the IRC, even though on the date of his death the decedent did not own any of the incidents of ownership.

General Information Regarding Life Insurance

As a product, life insurance has some interesting philosophical contradictions. If the insured dies prematurely, life insurance is a great investment and a windfall that may return many times the amount of the premiums invested in the policy. However, if the insured significantly outlives the mortality predicted in the actuarial tables used by insurance companies in determining premiums, life insurance might turn out to be a terrible investment. Yet if each of us had our choice, everyone would prefer a long life and a poor investment to the windfall of a premature death. Since life expectancies have increased dramatically in recent decades, the insurance companies have prospered by the medical advances in our society.

Life insurance is a very important part of planning an estate. The effective use of life insurance can provide your family with significant assets that are outside your taxable estate and with the liquid assets to pay estate taxes without being compelled to sell assets upon short notice. There are countless stories of individuals who have built significant enterprises during their lifetimes which had to be sold on their death in order to pay estate taxes. Life insurance enables beneficiaries to sell such enterprises when the time is right, not necessarily at the time of your death.

This book will not explain the numerous different types of policies, e.g. term, whole life, universal life and variable life, nor will we address in this book other important subjects, such as group insurance, insurance to fund buy-sell agreements, tax-free exchanges of life insurance policies, life settlements, stranger-owned life insurance, and many others. Make sure you consult a qualified and competent insurance agent who can address the many insurance products available and the strategies, as well as providing you with the best deal.

Life insurance can be purchased in a form that will allow the death benefit proceeds to bypass and not be included in your gross estate. The simplest way of achieving this is to have the purchase made by another individual or a trust for the benefit of others, usually descendants. Sometimes it is advisable that the insured own the policy even though the proceeds will be included in the gross estate. By owning the life insurance policy, the insured will retain the ability to access the cash surrender value if these funds are needed to supplement retirement income. Although the proceeds will be included in the decedent's gross estate, the decedent can pass these to the surviving spouse, or a marital trust for the surviving spouse, and escape immediate taxation.

ILITs, Split-Dollar and Second-to-Die

The typical technique for avoiding estate inclusion is for an irrevocable life insurance trust (an "ILIT") to purchase the policy (or to transfer an existing policy to an ILIT, subject to the 3-year holding period requirement of IRC Section 2035). The steps are:

CHAPTER VII – LIFE INSURANCE

- First, prepare the ILIT that probably will be a trust for the benefit of descendants;

- Second, make sure the ILIT has an independent trustee (who can be a spouse or descendant of the insured) since the decedent cannot act as trustee or retain incidents of ownership by himself or together with another;

- Third, provide for the payment of the insurance premiums by the ILIT, which can be accomplished by an initial gift to the ILIT within the insured's lifetime exemption or, even better, by annual gifts that are sheltered by a "Crummey" power in the ILIT that allows the annual gifts to qualify for the annual exclusion.

So-called "split-dollar arrangements" are another widely-used technique. Split-dollar allows a sharing of the costs and benefits. Typically, a family-owned corporation will make most or all of the premium payments as a loan, an ILIT will own the policy and, upon the death of the insured the ILIT will receive the proceeds, repay the loan, and distribute the balance to descendants of the insured. Although there are IRS tables that specify the amount that is required to be allocated to the insured as compensation or a gift and IRS regulations issued in 2003 that significantly reduced the benefits of the split-dollar arrangement, the split-dollar arrangement continues to be popular.

Another popular approach is to purchase a "second-to-die" policy that insures two lives, usually both spouses, paying the death benefit upon the death of the second to die. Premiums for a second-to-die policy usually are considerably lower than those applicable to a purchase of a single-life policy on each of the two spouses. Further, since federal estate taxes usually are deferred until the death of the second spouse through use of the unlimited marital deduction, the life insurance proceeds from a second-to-die policy will be received at the time needed to pay estate taxes.

CHAPTER VII – LIFE INSURANCE

Utilizing an ILIT and Crummey powers to pay premiums that are within the annual exclusion, the second-to-die policy usually is structured to be outside of the gross estate of both spouses and in an amount sufficient to pay all estate and inheritance taxes. Thus, the heirs will continue to have about the same amount of wealth as that of the two decedents, even after the payment of all death taxes. Second-to-die policies usually contain a rider allowing the policy to be divided into two single life policies in the event the married couple divorce.

We do not pretend to address all of the variations and different insurance products available, but there are many competent insurance agents whose expertise is essential in structuring a sound life insurance program.

Chapter VIII

RETIREMENT ACCOUNTS

Overview of Retirement Accounts

Retirement accounts for individuals can be classified as follows:

1. <u>Qualified Retirement Plans</u>. Below is a list of some of the most widely-used qualified retirement plans established by employers:

> (a) Profit sharing plan and money purchase pension plan;
>
> (b) Defined benefit pension plan;
>
> (c) Employee stock ownership plan ("ESOP");
>
> (d) Keogh plan for self-employed participants, i.e. proprietors and partners;
>
> (e) Section 401(k) plan, which is probably the most popular, under which the employer and employee both contribute.

CHAPTER VIII – RETIREMENT ACCOUNTS

In general, a qualified retirement plan established by an employer must not discriminate between the benefits earned by highly-compensated employees and non-highly-compensated employees. For qualified retirement plans established by an employer, the employer is allowed an income tax deduction for its contribution to the plan, even though the employee is not at that time required to recognize taxable income on the amount allocated to the employee/participant's account. The trust or other vehicle used by the plan to hold assets typically is tax-exempt, resulting in no income tax on the dividends, interest, other income and capital gains realized by the trust. The employee will not recognize taxable income until distribution of his account, and this can be further deferred by rolling over the distribution to an Individual Retirement Account ("IRA") or another qualified retirement plan of a new employer.

2. <u>Nonqualified Deferred Compensation Plans</u>. A nonqualified deferred compensation ("NDC") plan is a plan providing for payment of deferred compensation, usually intended to provide supplementary benefits for highly-compensated employees beyond those that can be provided under the nondiscriminatory rules applicable to qualified retirement plans. An NDC plan will not qualify for the favorable income tax benefits applicable to employers and employees under a qualified retirement plan, but an NDC plan can be designed in a variety of different ways to meet the requirements of specified individuals or groups of employees who are highly compensated. A typical NDC plan will have risks of forfeiture and other specified provisions that cannot be used in a qualified retirement plan. Under a qualified retirement plan, spousal consent is necessary if the designated beneficiary is an individual other than the spouse. No spousal consent is required for NDC plans.

3. <u>Individual Retirement Account ("IRA") and Roth IRA</u>. An individual may establish an IRA pursuant to which he can for

income tax purposes deduct annual contributions ($5,500 for 2014, or $6,500 if the individual is over age 50), but as a practical matter, the deduction is phased out and often eliminated if, for example, the adjusted gross income of the individual and the spouse is in excess of a specified amount ($181,000 for 2014). Nondeductible Roth IRAs were established for 1998 and subsequent years. Although there is no current income tax deduction for contributions to a Roth IRA, distributions from a Roth IRA are not subject to income tax. For an ordinary IRA, a distributee must include the distribution as taxable income unless the distributee can qualify for a rollover.

The many specific rules and limitations applicable to qualified retirement plans, NDC plans, IRAs and Roth IRAs for the most part are directed toward income tax considerations, e.g. deductibility of contributions and includability of distributions. The income tax rules applicable to these widely-used plans, in our opinion, are among the most detailed and complicated to be found in the IRC. The balance of this chapter will focus on estate planning issues applicable to these plans.

Estate Planning Considerations

The most important estate planning consideration applicable to retirement plan benefits, irrespective of whether they arise from a qualified retirement plan, an NDC plan, an IRA or a Roth IRA, is who should be the designated beneficiary in the event of the death of the participant. This issue needs to be periodically reviewed and updated, since the appropriate beneficiary designation changes from time to time. Often the participant makes the designation of his beneficiary when presented with a form from his employer or investment advisor, at which time the participant may not have a well-constructed estate plan.

Below are alternatives for designating beneficiaries:

CHAPTER VIII – RETIREMENT ACCOUNTS

- <u>Surviving Spouse</u>. Bear in mind that a spousal <u>consent is necessary if the primary beneficiary</u> under a qualified retirement plan is someone other than the surviving spouse. In most cases, the participant's surviving spouse should be the beneficiary. In addition to avoiding the necessary spousal consent, this will provide the participant with a marital deduction for estate tax purposes and permit the spouse to roll over the account into his or her own IRA, which often will result in significant income tax deferral.

- <u>A Marital Trust for the Benefit of the Surviving Spouse</u>. Using a QTIP trust defers payment of the estate tax until death of the surviving spouse but allows the participant to designate who receives the funds on the death of the surviving spouse, e.g. children from a prior marriage.

- <u>A Nonmarital Trust</u>. This is intended to utilize the participant's unused lifetime exemption (presently $5,340,000). This is generally used in cases where a participant does not have sufficient other assets to fund the nonmarital or credit shelter trust.

- <u>Children or Other Descendants</u>. This can be left either outright or in trust.

- <u>Charities</u>. Up to $100,000 per year can be distributed from a traditional or Roth IRA of an individual over 70½ years of age and will be excluded from adjusted gross income if distributed directly to a charity. Even though the individual is not permitted to deduct the amount given to charity, the individual can avoid the impact of limitations that reduce deductions if the adjusted gross income of the individual and the spouse exceeds certain levels. For example, this is a desirable technique if the donor's charitable contributions will exceed 50% of

CHAPTER VIII – RETIREMENT ACCOUNTS

adjusted gross income or if the donor does not itemize deductions.

Other Applicable Principles

It bears remembering that under the terms of applicable bankruptcy laws all of the benefits from qualified retirement plans (even if they are rolled into an IRA) and up to $1.0 million of an IRA account are exempt from and are not part of the bankruptcy estate. Thus, these are protected from claims of creditors.

Receipt of distributions from a qualified retirement plan, an NDC plan or a traditional IRA can be subject to both estate taxes (unless protected by the marital deduction or lifetime exemption) and federal income taxes, since payments received from qualified and nonqualified deferred compensation plans are taxable as ordinary income in respect of the decedent ("IRD"). Although for federal income tax purposes the recipient is allowed a deduction for the federal estate taxes paid, this deduction, which is not the same as a credit, will not fully recoup the federal estate tax paid nor will it recoup any part of state death tax paid. Thus, in instances where the individual and the spouse will have a large taxable estate and a large amount of IRD, it is advisable to direct the IRD to the surviving spouse so that the federal income tax attributable to the IRD will reduce the taxable estate and resulting estate taxes due upon the death of the surviving spouse.

It is worth noting that Illinois and many other states do not impose a state income tax on distributions from qualified retirement plans. It is open to conjecture whether these states are doing so to protect their senior residents, who are an important voting group, or to persuade this group to refrain from moving to another state that does not have a state income tax.

If benefits of retirement plans are large, be very careful in your planning since the applicable income and estate tax

CHAPTER VIII – RETIREMENT ACCOUNTS

provisions are like a mine field, where every step must be perfect in order to avoid a disastrous explosion.

CHAPTER IX

A POTPOURRI OF OTHER WEAPONS IN YOUR ARSENAL

The income, gift and estate tax laws, in our view, resemble a war between the government, on one hand, and wealthy individuals, on the other hand. First, Illinois residents who achieve the highest income tax bracket pay an income tax of between 25% (20% on capital gains plus state income tax) and 50% (44% on ordinary income plus state income tax). If the remaining balance of your wealth exceeds $10.7 million, the federal estate tax of 40% and the Illinois estate tax of about 16% (but deductible for purposes of calculating the federal estate tax) will claim approximately 50% of the remainder. Thus, the tax laws have decreed that the federal and state governments, in effect, are partners in your wealth—they own a majority interest—and that if you are passive in your action to prevent this, taxes will consume most of your lifetime earnings and accumulations in excess of the lifetime exemption.

But the tax laws also have provided you with an arsenal of weapons that you can use in this war. The prior chapters of this book have explained some of the more important weapons in

CHAPTER IX – A POUTPOURRI OF OTHER WEAPONS IN YOUR ARSENAL

your arsenal. This chapter will briefly explain a medley of other weapons you have or, if you prefer less aggressive terminology than "weapons" and "war," the "steps" that you can "take in order to reduce your taxes." In the 1935 tax decision, <u>Helvering v. Gregory</u>, a very prominent jurist, Judge Learned Hand, made this often-quoted pronouncement:

> "Any one may so arrange his affairs that his taxes shall be as low as possible; he is not bound to choose the pattern which will best pay the Treasury; there is not even a patriotic duty to increase one's taxes."

Avoiding State Income and Inheritance Taxes

State income taxes vary, with top rates widely ranging from 13.3% in California, 12.7% in New York City and 5% in Illinois, to zero in a number of states, e.g. Florida, Texas and Wyoming. Florida does not have any estate or inheritance tax, and since the prohibition of income and death taxes is mandated by the Florida Constitution, no change can occur unless the citizens of Florida amend their Constitution, an event that will not occur. Thus, significant income tax and death tax savings are possible simply by changing your residence to Florida.

Many individuals believe that a change of residency requires that you spend more than six months in the newly-chosen state of residency. That is not correct. The determination of residency is based on your intention—in which state you <u>intend</u> to reside—but this is determined by objective factors. It is generally advisable that you not be present in the former state of residence for more than six months. Thus, since many wealthy individuals will travel to places other than the former and the newly-chosen states of residence, spending six months in the newly-chosen state is not a requirement, but being away from the former state of residence for more than six months is advisable.

CHAPTER IX – A POUTPOURRI OF OTHER WEAPONS IN YOUR ARSENAL

There are other steps that one should take to objectively establish that he or she intended to change the state of residence. Below are the more important of the other steps necessary to change your residence from Illinois to Florida:

- File Florida Declaration of Domicile with Clerk of Circuit Court of county of residence

- Automobile:
    Obtain Florida driver's license
    Obtain Florida license plates for vehicle

- Register to vote in Florida

- File for Florida homestead exemption for residence, but you will need to relinquish Illinois Homestead Exemption going forward

- Open Florida bank account

- Change credit cards to Florida address

- Use non-resident memberships for clubs in Illinois and resident memberships for clubs in Florida

- Sign new Will and Trust Agreement reflecting residence in Florida

Disclaimers

A disclaimer is a refusal by a donee or a legatee to accept a gift or a bequest. A "qualified disclaimer" is the irrevocable and unqualified written refusal to accept this interest made within nine months from the date of the transfer. The result of a qualified disclaimer is that the property transferred will be

CHAPTER IX – A POUTPOURRI OF OTHER WEAPONS IN YOUR ARSENAL

received by a person other than the disclaimant without any gift or taxable transfer by the disclaimant.

The qualified disclaimer is an important post-mortem planning tool that can be used to alter ill-advised dispositive provisions of a document. Heirs can use a disclaimer to rewrite a decedent's will. Assume that the testator, a wealthy individual, leaves her estate equally among her then living children, per stirpes. Testator has two children, a son, who is very wealthy, and a daughter, who is not. The wealthy son can execute a qualified disclaimer allowing his one-half of the estate to pass to his children without this constituting a taxable gift. If the wealthy son does not disclaim, he will have to incur a gift tax or an estate tax in order to achieve a transfer to his children.

If the residue of the testator's estate is left to a charity, including a private foundation, a qualified disclaimer by the legatees can be utilized to increase the charitable deduction and thereby minimize estate taxes.

There are many other uses of a qualified disclaimer to rearrange disposition of assets that are transferred by gift, under a will or testamentary trust, pursuant to a beneficiary designation under a life insurance policy or retirement plan, and pursuant to the laws applicable to joint tenancies and community property. Sometimes it is necessary to have successive disclaimers to accomplish the desired objective. All of the successive disclaimers must be made within the same nine-month period.

Although qualified disclaimers can repair improperly drafted estate planning documents or can change properly drafted documents that no longer are suitable due to changing times or circumstances, the better alternative is for the estate planner to make sure that the documents accomplish the most advantageous objectives so that no disclaimer is necessary.

CHAPTER IX – A POUTPOURRI OF OTHER WEAPONS IN YOUR ARSENAL

Gifts to Minors

Gifts to a minor under the age of 21 present a set of tax and non-tax considerations that differ from those applicable to adults.

The tax incentive for gifts to minors arises principally from the desire to fully utilize the $28,000 annual exclusion for each donee that is available to a married couple. Bear in mind that this exclusion is for each year for each donee. This $28,000 annual exclusion for each grandchild and great-grandchild can result in substantial reductions in the estate tax, generation-skipping transfer tax, and also in income taxes if the so-called "Kiddie Tax," which we will subsequently explain, can be avoided.

The customary forms for making gifts to minors of the $28,000 annual exclusion are:

- Transfer the property to a parent of the minor to hold it under the Uniform Transfers to Minors Act ("UTMA").

- Transfer the property to a so-called Section 2503(c) trust. Use of this trust is generally considered preferable to a transfer under the UTMA since the UTMA transfer will require giving the property to the minor at age 21, but the 2503(c) trust permits retention in the trust beyond age 21, if the minor is given the right to withdraw in a 30-day window upon attaining the age of 21.

- Transfer the property to a trust that has Crummey powers that the minor, acting through his parent, can exercise, but which generally are waived and not exercised.

In addition to being able to gift $28,000 each year to each donee, a donor can pay the tuition (but not books, supplies, room and board) directly to an "educational institution" without this being treated as a taxable gift. An "education institution" includes

CHAPTER IX – A POUTPOURRI OF OTHER WEAPONS IN YOUR ARSENAL

all public and private schools for the primary grades, high school, college undergraduate programs, and graduate schools. Nursery and pre-school day care programs also might qualify as educational expenses.

An individual also is allowed an unlimited gift tax exclusion for amounts paid on behalf of an individual directly to a provider of medical care, including for medical insurance. Be careful not to permit the donee to pay the medical expense since reimbursement to the donee will not qualify for the exclusion.

Kiddie Tax

The so-called "Kiddie Tax" taxes unearned income (i.e. investment income) at the parents' highest marginal tax rate. Before enactment of this statute that became effective in 1987, a minor child's unearned income was taxed at the child's rate. That accomplished a substantial income tax savings and encouraged the transfer of income-producing assets to minors.

The Kiddie Tax applies if the child is:

- under the age of 18 at the end of the tax year;

- under the age of 19 at the end of the tax year and does not provide more than half of his or her own support with earned income;

- under the age of 24 at the end of the tax year, a full-time student, and does not provide more than half of his or her own support with earned income.

"Special Needs" Trusts for Disabled Individuals

There are special problems applicable to a disabled individual who is receiving or may need to receive benefits from

CHAPTER IX – A POUTPOURRI OF OTHER WEAPONS IN YOUR ARSENAL

governmental agencies, e.g. Medicaid or SSI. These governmental agencies generally provide beneficiaries with funds, but only in amounts sufficient to obtain "necessities." The objective is to allow a disabled beneficiary to simultaneously continue to receive the assistance provided by the governmental agencies and, in addition, to receive benefits from a "special needs" trust that provides the beneficiary with the comforts in excess of the "necessities" that the governmental agencies provide.

We only briefly mention some of the many different individuals that might be served by a special needs trust, e.g. one created by the settlor for himself, a third-party created "special needs" trust, a "special needs" trust for an individual who resides in a medical facility, a "special needs" trust established to receive a personal injury or other litigation settlement. The subject is complex. In addition to tax and financial considerations, analysis is required as to how to provide for the proper care of the individual and how to avoid disrupting the benefits being received from governmental agencies. An in-depth analysis of a special needs trust is beyond the purview of this book. The critical part of a "special needs" trust is to avoid mandatory distributions to the beneficiary that will disrupt benefits from governmental agencies and, at the same time, provide the trustee with discretion to use the funds of the trust to provide benefits and assistance to the beneficiary, but only in excess of the "necessities" that are provided under the governmental assistance programs.

Still More Weapons in Taxpayer's Arsenal

We only briefly mention a few of the many other tax savings techniques that are available to the estate planner: grantor retained annuity trusts ("GRATs"); private annuities; self-cancelling installment notes; and qualified personal residence trusts ("QPRTs"). An estate planner also deals with a host of special problems: asset protection planning; community property; income taxation of estates and trusts; duties and

CHAPTER IX – A POUTPOURRI OF OTHER WEAPONS IN YOUR ARSENAL

responsibilities of fiduciaries; trust decanting; problems of non-citizens and estate and gift tax treaties with foreign countries; U.S. taxation of foreign estates, trusts and beneficiaries; operations of private foundations and public charities; probate administration of estates and trusts; and ante-nuptial agreements. We leave all of these matters to a possible subsequent book.

CONCLUSION

As we put the finishing touches on this book, we reflect on what is the important message that we want to communicate to our readers. We introduced this message at the beginning of Chapter IX: that wealthy individuals are engaged in a war—or certainly a gigantic struggle—with federal and state governments over the disposition of wealth upon their death. Although you are battling a Goliath, the Goliath is passive and cannot initiate strategic moves other than revising the laws. You, however, can be a resourceful strategist and implement your objectives with the numerous weapons in your arsenal.

David slew Goliath utilizing strategic weapons, a sling and stone. You have an assortment of many weapons. Your task as a warrior is to read this book carefully and try to understand the many strategic techniques that are available. We urge you to acquire knowledge so that you can be an active participant with your estate planner in formulating an estate plan that slays, or significantly weakens, the Goliath that you are confronting.

www.ingramcontent.com/pod-product-compliance
Lightning Source LLC
Chambersburg PA
CBHW071803170526
45167CB00003B/1146